MW00880057

THE KILL MANUAL

Anna Childs

Cover Photograph by Steven Wang

ISBN: 9781797072197
Imprint: Independently published

you didn't plan for a life after misery. there was only one torturous moment after the next and then the end. you planned for your future in terms of loss, and fear, and regret. it was cavernous and cancerous and you carried it like a nest deep inside of you. but the same way winter eventually loses its grip on the sky, and the same way hurricanes eventually lose their grip on the sea, that same darkness lost its grip on you. the world saved you with bits and pieces of light, one helping hand, after another smiling face. you discovered hearts and met people just as kind, and gracious, and sensitive as you. until one day that black nest deep inside of you sprouted leaves, and blossomed flowers, and soon enough you had accumulated a garden's worth of love and healing. you found understanding, purpose, and peace.

so maybe you didn't plan for a life after misery. but life already had its plans for you.

In loving memory of
all the moments, people, and places
we'll never see again.

THE KILL MANUAL

INIQUITY

THE KILL MANUAL

We rolled off the bed,
onto the floor,
when he put his
hand to my throat
and told me
he could only love me
if I admitted he could kill me,

so I laughed,
thinking it was a joke,

he did not
let me go.

I don’t make love,
I make mistakes.

The pregnancy will twist you,
morph you,
force you,
into a person
you were not ready
to become.

Your soul shatters,
cracks and breaks
at the way he slams
your ultrasound photo
onto the cold table
of the diner
you're mourning over
like two gods
who have misused
their power to create.

– *Nine Weeks, Six Days*

We are all guilty
of something.

All gods
are lonely creatures.

The room hangs dark
like bad decisions at 3 a.m.
when you awaken
next to his warm body in bed,
strangers passed out
like drugs and loose cigarettes
on the floor,
broken like every promise
and the first condom
you ever begged him to wear,

there is nothing for your soul here,
yet you keep coming back
as if lost people
could ever find one another.

This is how he plans
to keep the pinky promise
he makes you,

the night he stays out
until morning
trading bags of drugs
for money
to take you to the doctor.

– No One Ever Wants to Be That Story

We all need breaks,
even from the things we love.

The Clinic

You've never liked these paper gowns
and that still hasn't changed,
the way the doctor pries
your legs open
like a mausoleum,
his ancient face fluorescent
white like the lights
buzzing overhead,
in this place
where so many things
come to die,

you are alone in more ways
you ever thought you could be.

You hadn't begged
anyone for anything,
never fought or feared
for your own life,
until the morning came
your mother found you

hands shaking,
eyes fluttering,
red gushing
down your legs,

the way she stood there
in horror shrieking,

ripping out fistfuls of hair,
falling to her knees,
pleading.

– *Call the Ambulance*

She traps you
in your bedroom,

but the pain
is getting worse,

so she listens to you
vomit water

on the inside
of your shirt.

You are begging,
screaming, praying
to the empty walls,

hoping someone
will hear you,

anyone at all.

– PLEASE

You need a hospital
but they laugh

when they hear you
scream,

they tell you
this is what shameful girls deserve,

you're a *whore,*
a *slut,*
a *beast.*

the day your mother finds out about your abortion, the way you're taking shelter in your room, afraid, terrified of what she might do. howling and chanting. for once. your mother brings her church friend over, some lady you never knew, to drag you out of bed by the womb. bleeding and screaming. *this is how you repent,* they said. you're supposed to be on bed rest and you're too weak to stand. that day nobody will be home to help you. dizzy and weak and grovelling at their feet. your fingers smeared red like the inside of your legs. hot liquid streaks dragged like iron crosses. crucified and nailed against the hardwood floor. kicking and screaming and begging for peace. until the police. the paramedics. the flashing images of red lights and sirens mourning down your street. your mother handcuffed, restrained, howling what would've been your child's name. with her church friend. who helped kill every soft part of you that day.

She left you to die,
you needed her
more than anything
and she left you to die.

– *Mommy*

We hear the stories of absent fathers,
men who left us with no last names,
emotionally crippled,
violent and abusive in nature.
I did not know my real father either,
a man with my rage and angry face,
my mother says,
a man who ran off and died
fighting in another man's war
as my step-father took his place.
I will probably never know
how to solve the other half
of the equation to who I am,
but some strange, invisible man
is not, has not, and never will be
the reason I cannot not stand,

it was my mother,

I watched pieces of her wilt,
shatter and fall away
every single day
of my entire life.

– *Inherited Pain*

My mother broke my heart
long before any man
ever laid a hand on me.

Mom writes you letters,
scribbled loving bruises
in red and pink crayon
from the psychiatric ward,

she does not regret,
has no remorse,
does not remember
what she has done.

– *Psychosis*

Being raised by a parent
suffering from mental illness
is coming home
to a different person
every day.

– *Never Knowing Who to Expect*

Her mother sends her
to ten years' worth of catholic classes,
a little girl in a plaid skirt
standing before the eyes of judgment,
scripture engraved like tombstones
scorched into her itchy skin
where they teach her
the seven deadly sins of her lonely heart,
that women are the downfall of men,
that her body is shameful,
and that the little piece of paradise
she keeps warm between her legs
holds enough power to bring
even the mightiest God himself
down to his knees.

– *And They Wonder Where She Learned It*

I was once so soft,
so quiet and small,
shrinking myself,
taking up no space at all,

until they took
a razor to my skin.

– Scraped Me Pink and Raw

You have spent
the entirety of your life
being told you are *too sensitive*,
inconvenient, and unwanted,
a person unworthy
of being cared for,

you open yourself up
ripe like the gates of heaven

to the first person
who makes you feel
anything holy.

"Your body is not
your temple,"

my mother says.

"Your body is
more like a morgue.

How will any man
ever love you again?"

– I Don't Know

That same old Mustang pulls up
like a pumpkin carriage
to the front steps
of your apartment building
when he asks
if you've ever had car sex,

you wonder if this is how
Cinderella lost her glass slipper.

You let him grip you
as hard as he wants,
bending you over
his torn-up couch,

this is how
you confuse fucking
for making love.

– 4 A.M.

You have always felt punished
for wanting more,

always stupid
for needing them
as badly as you do.

You treat sex
like a bandage

when sex
is the wound.

The clock strikes 3 p.m.,
you're seated around a large table
with your entire family
and this reminds you
of every meal
you've never eaten together.

Your mom's psychiatrist asks,
"How do we fix what has become broken?"

To which you reply,
"We don't."

– *Nothing Has Ever Been Whole*

Your sister can't look you
in the eyes anymore
and you never knew
how much this could hurt,

to have someone you love
refuse to meet you
at the doors of your soul.

We raised each other
and I'm sorry

I couldn't be
the love

or the mother
we both deserved

but I promise you,
I tried,

god,
did I try.

– *Sisters*

Some roles can never be replaced,
no matter how hard we strive
to fill the empty space.

We are at each other's throats
when we should be
in each other's hearts.

You are drowning out the world
in the mess of his living room,
eyes rolling back, drinking to forget,
when he asks how your father's doing,
"How's the cancer?" he says,
offering you a bump of white powder
that bakes brains like flour,
flipping the black wires of his slick hair
back against the walls,
he winks, "To take the edge off."

But you refuse,
lowering the whiskey bottle
from your lips, you tell him
the edge means nothing
when your life is a cliff

and cancer, well,
it's a bitch.

There is no resurrection
at the bottom of a bottle,
no redemption
in the drugs or empty sex,

your heart is only begging,
attempting to forget.

– *Self-Medication*

You are searching
for cures

in places where
people only get sick.

You starved yourself
to be skinny enough
so he'd be hungry enough
for more,

until your heart had turned
to skin and bones
and your jeans fell
to the floor.

You feel too big
for your own arms

so you look
for somebody else
to hold you.

The same hands that carried you home
that night you blacked out
in the alley,

are the same hands that helped you
find all of your classes
the first day of college,

are the same hands that held you
face down against the mattress,
shattering the stained-glass windows
between your legs,

turning your insides to shards
so broken and hard,
you cried yourself numb
to the pain.

My body has done things
I never knew it was capable of,

and I have accessed parts of myself
I never thought existed.

– *Womanhood*

Abuse twists us
purple

until the only colour
we can see is
black.

When we hear the word *abuse*
we paint pictures of bruised faces,
moonlit eyes and cherry lips,
my father hit me good as a kid
but I still cannot salvage
the nuclear damage radiating from his words,
half-lives I never understood
how someone could beat me down
without touching me at all,
how a person could break my heart
without breaking any skin,
how a man could ruin me
without leaving any scars,
most days my face wasn't bruised,
my heart was,
and every time my father promised me
he did not love me,

I always wished he
had just hit me instead.

They beat you
with the same hands
meant to love you,

this is not the way
love should hurt.

You are ten years old
when your dad
grabs a fistful of soft hair
from the back of your scalp,
ripping it like hot wax,
dragging your
ankles hardly touching the floor
when he throws you
into the foyer,
calls you a cocksucker,
kicks you, spits,
and slams the door.

You are quiet and forgiving
in the face of malice
when you shouldn't be,

you are hard and rejecting
in the face of love
when you shouldn't be.

The people who raise you
are responsible for setting the standard
as to how you should be respected,
cared for and treated,
so when you talk over your five-year old,
ignore your seven-year old,
beat down your sixteen-year old daughter,
remember you are creating
some of the first acts of violence
in another person's life,
replacing love with pain
inside of a little heart
that only knows
everything you are failing to teach it.

All of the pain
feels like love,

but it's not.

We do nasty things
to the people we hate,

nastier things
to the people we love.

Love is the greatest of all disciplines.

You are too depressed and empty to do anything but cry
and sex is only a reminder of all your mistakes,
he acts like he doesn't need you now
because he doesn't need you,
he's already moved on
to someone else,
he left you
with nothing,
lost inside your head
to a womb so horribly haunted,
forgotten like ghosts and early graves,
there is nothing to show for anything now,
the world took, and it took, and it took, and so did he.

– *Everything Else Is Gone*

His problem is he falls in love
with every girl he meets,

he loved me
and he loved you too.

– For A Second

Promises are not
meant to be
broken.

You think about
killing yourself
more often than not,
you don’t want to die
but the trauma haunts you,
chokes you,
never fucking stops.

The anxiety attacks
sink you in waves,
oceanic storms crashing,
tearing open your treasure chest,
megatons of pressure
squeezing your lungs,
your heart swollen
doubloons of blue and red,
the nurses run wires,
tape machines to your breasts,
you are fighting to leave this world,
to bring your suffering to an end.

You craved an escape route,
a way out of the planetary burden
forced upon your shoulders,
clinging to the first person as if
sex was the obvious answer,
the only source of relief
in the anarchy of your universe
where nooses hang like umbilical chords,
pretending to be in love
for the sake of having something to do,
forging pacts of regret
written in each other's names,
crashing helplessly
into the wanting arms of strangers
without asking any questions,
as us lonely and desperate people usually do
in the absence of ourselves.

I am losing myself
to death.

Your best friend of ten years
comes back home from California
to pieces of you missing,
fragmented the way your smile
still shines with him,
sitting in your kitchen
laughing back your stories of trauma
like apologetic shots of make believe,
pretending everything is fine
as your voice cracks,
as your words fester and bleed,
proving you have nothing left to lose
is the night he tells you he loves you.

He kissed your shaking hands
like the medicine you so desperately needed,
laying there, half-naked in bed,
his glossy eyes pouring over
the rounded shoulders of your soul,
he says, "I promise never to leave you
alone like that ever again."

"I will always be here,"
He says.

"It's just you and me now,"
He says.

"I love you,"
He says.

"You are not the same anymore,"
He says.

"You feel broken,"
He says.
"Let me fix you."

he will be the first man you allow back inside what's left of your body, the sarcophagus of your being, sweeping through catacombs of regret and dust, your eyes bagged like ravaged beds of sleepy purple violets and hands spread hot like wildfire over the stitches in your soul. he will say that even at your worst you are beautiful. you have always been so disastrously beautiful in the mirrors of his broken jungle eyes. cracked and tearing at your clothes like years' worth of laughter and tension finally reaching molecular blasts of lightning and sweet, god damn release. every ripple of wanting lost in the crashing tidal waves of bed sheets, looming over his hurricane-blue lips. the threat of total and complete destruction. and you will believe all of the promises in his voice. vulnerable like people in this world really should be. whispering memories like highlight reels of fairy tale rhymes. a broken childhood past. skies that will never look the same again.

this is how he pretends to be your friend. your life saver. pulling you from the brinks of death only because he himself was not finished with you yet. not wholly quenched. and no, my dear, he is not god sent. he is a vulture. he does not want you, he only wants what's left of you. the rotten apple core of iniquity between your legs.

– The People We Never Hear from Again (A Lifelong Friend)

Everything
has become
pain,

even the numb
hurts.

You can't help but feel as if you have failed,
fucked up your life, fighting off good decisions
with the jagged edges of broken whiskey bottles,
blowing smoke in the face of love
and flipping off the sun because
how dare it rise another painful day,
illuminating the monsters hidden in your dark,
casting shadows against your bagged eyes,
forcing sleeplessness from you, so everyone can see
just how horrible you look under the light,
"Yes, this is my face," you want to say,
"It is tired, and angry, and scarred,
and this face once belonged to a person
with hopes and dreams."
Before life crushed the breath from their ribs,
ripped the truth from their throats,
and scraped the happiness from their smiles.
Is this how villains are born?
The venomous remains of people
who've had love stolen from them
time and time again,
so they wait for the day
where the world no longer turns,
where the universe no longer exists,
spitting on every broken star in the sky,
cursing God's name,
screaming into the heavens, begging
WHY, WHY, WHY?

You suffer for everyone,
hold space for everyone,
forgive and love
and make an effort
to help everyone.

But who suffers for you?
Who fights for you?

Who stays
and waits
and wishes
for you?

You never liked these funny games
fate always seems to play
so you climbed up over the streets,
to meet death face to face.

– *Rooftops*

I look over
the cliff of my thoughts
and realize I'm scared of heights,

or maybe I'm just scared
I'll fall.

I did not leave a note.

– I Was Too Broken to Write

The thought of losing
one more person

is enough to paint
the sidewalk red,

but in this moment
something clicks.

– *You'd Lose Everyone If You Were Dead*

And they would
lose you,
too.

Even after everything,
nobody could have
ever hurt you

the way that you were
about to hurt yourself.

You have been so desperate for a way out,
but the answer does not lay
in your destruction.

DO

NOT

ABANDON

YOURSELF

You never placed any value
or importance on yourself
and in that same light failed to realize
how your own self-destructive behaviours,
toxic relationships and neglectful choices
affected those around you,
you didn't think anyone cared
about what you did,
where you went,
if you even came home,
but the truth is
the people who really do love you
will always be subject to your actions,
how you treat yourself,
what you choose to say,
because in their hearts you matter
and they too will be gone someday.

– *Love and Letters to Myself*

Your life is precious,
no matter what anyone says,
does, or makes you think,

hold onto yourself
with everything you have,

never give yourself up
to the opinions and actions
of those who live to break you.

Please
do not confuse
suicide with solution,
taking your own life
will never be the answer.
I love you,
whoever you are,
you in all of your light,
you in all of your sorrow,
whoever you are right now
reading these words on this page,
I wrote all of this because I love you.

You are the miracle
you have been waiting for,
I promise.

– *Anna*

ISOLATION

Scars remind us
that although we survived
we are not invincible.

– Collateral Damage

You tore the clothes like excess skin
from your body,
let the scalding shower water
hammer over the soft spot
on your scalp,
fistfuls of matted knots
in a whirlpool of torn hair
spiraling down the metallic vortex
of the drain,
each scab on your face
peeling like wet wallpaper,
stinging raw beneath
the burning onslaught of pain,

"All of those things
I have always done for other people,
why have I never done any of that for myself?"

The day you chose
not to jump

was the day you knew
the only way out
was through.

This will not be easy,
saving yourself
means taking a sword
to the throat of every monster
that has ever followed you home,

confronting every nightmare,
bad feeling and horrid truth
you have ever ignored.

This pain will be
the greatest of any.

If I want to be
the person I want to be

I'm going to have to stop
being so afraid of heights,
of depths, of love, of life,

and most importantly
I'm going to have to stop
being so afraid of myself.

You saved every last penny,
packed your world into bags,
scoured the city for boxes,
left home in search of home.

You don’t know
what it’s like to be alone,

you have never enjoyed
being in the company
of yourself,

you and yourself
are not even friends.

You have always filled
your empty spaces with people,
the silent air with any conversation
anyone was ever willing to have,
music, and noise, and tv's left on
just so you wouldn't have to think,
hiding the wars behind smiles,
silly jokes, and ongoing laughter,
never telling any of your friends,
and although some of these
have not been the worst coping mechanisms
the time has finally come
for you to be alone with yourself,
to face the silence
you have spent so long
pretending wasn't there.

I have been alone
for a very long time now,

different kinds of alone,
at different points in time.

I am siphoning the venom
from my life,
plucking each and every
flesh eating lie
and bitter thorn,

there is no more room
for toxic people.

– *No More Space in My Soul*

You have taken an axe
to every tree in your forest

just to build people
the kind of homes you never had.

The only reason you feel
the world has failed you
is because you have put
all of the right faith
into the wrong people.

– *And None into Yourself*

I am not looking for revenge,
the way destroyed people
destroyed me
to no end,

I am
looking for forgiveness,
a way to heal myself and others
so that maybe one day I'll understand.

The moment you decide
to hurt someone back
is the moment you become
all of the bad things
you have always disliked
about this world.

– *The Cycle*

Anger is destructive
and I cannot afford to keep
rebuilding my life.

Our hearts are all broken
yet we continue to be
reckless with one another
because we as a humanity
are creating new wounds
faster than we can heal
the old wounds.

There is no lack of intimacy,
I'm a very intimate person,
but there is an overwhelming
lack of trust,
of willingness,
of love.

You have always hidden
your depression
like a broken promise
behind your back,
the same way your mother hid
her own damaged pieces
from your father,
how he hated her
for everything she was not,
you are convinced
nobody will ever
love you again.

You do not answer the phone when she calls,
your mother's voice unloving you
with messages so threatening and vile
it makes you hate every cell
within your hair, skin, and legs,
every inch of your DNA,

forever fighting for your right to exist
amongst these pieces of her

reflected from within
the shattered mirror of your soul

every time you go
to wash your hands.

– *Imprisoned*

The darkness within me
is a familiar home.

You flinch like an abused animal
beneath gentle hands,
crying dangerously
in the arms of strangers,
one night stands you cannot stand
to follow through
without breaking down
explaining why it is
you can't have sex.

– *Relapse*

When something bad
happens to me
I’m a wreck,

when something good
happens to me
I’m a wreck.

You cannot handle
the idea of anything great
collapsing anymore,
the constant reminder
that all things come to an end,

you'd rather not have
anything at all.

It has become
physically impossible
to fill the void,

all of these people
only remind you
of how terribly
you hurt.

– *Casual Encounters*

But you don’t want
meaningful sex either,

meaningful sex
means a meaningful person

and a meaningful person
means the possibility
of losing everything
all over again.

I am continuously
on the run,

running from something,
running toward something,

you'd think my heart
would be in much better shape.

It's weird how time works,
one moment you're here,
the next moment you're there,

you're at work,
        you're at home,
                you're at school,

one moment
every molecule in your being
needs to be touched,

the next moment
you long to be left alone forever.

We reject what we cannot handle,
that is why some of us
reject love.

Love feels like the sun,
like a fantastic ball of light in the sky
not meant for me to touch.

The other night
I saw my entire life
unfold before me,

all of the things
I had convinced myself
I never wanted,

all of the things
I told myself
I'd never need,

they were all there,

they were all there
and I was with you.

You haven't found
a new person
to love yet

so you cling
to all of the people
you once knew.

I miss you
in all of the ways
you are not here.

I know nothing
lasts forever,

but it would be nice
to keep something
for just a little while.

I haven't been touched
in so long

it's like forgetting
the way your hands feel.

– *Everything Burns*

Your body's only job
is to keep you alive
but you have experienced
so much trauma,
blood, and death,
you fear these pieces
of yourself
may one day
turn against you too.

– *Eaten Alive*

All monsters
were once human.

Words mean nothing
at this point,

I only write
to keep myself
from going insane.

This is a process
you are not fucked up,
you are just healing.

– S.M.

I am all that I have,

it does not make me
love anyone any less,

it does not make me
love myself any more.

I still cannot write
about the pregnancy.

Some days I am so happy
I forget any reason
for ever being mad at
the world at all,

other days
my body cannot seem
to pick itself up
off the floor.

Anxiety
and depression
are the fatal symptoms
of a broken
heart.

I don’t think it’s important to understand
as much as it’s important to love,

I don’t need to be dissected,
I only wish to feel whole.

They told me it did not matter,
"You are young,"
they said.
"You will forget,
everyone always forgets."

It's been four years now,
four years and I still feel the same.

That's how trauma works,

everything around you
could be different

but nothing inside of
you has changed.

Our bodies can only stand
so much pain before they go numb,

we need to understand
our minds work the same way.

– *Mental Shock*

This is your new home,
the maze of forgotten memories,

where days become weeks,
weeks become years,

and you still
cannot remember a thing.

– *Repression*

Being lost within yourself
is the most dangerous kind of lost there is.

My mind
is not the same place
it once was.

I cannot
remember the person
I used to be.

Hell is every part of your heart
that has already died.

You don’t fight depression
with medications,

you fight it in a room,
alone,
every
day.

There is no greater sorrow
than watching the rest of the world
move on without you.

You did not just hit rock bottom,
you crashed through it,
crushed your bones against it,
peeled your skin to shreds
on its teeth,
drowning in pieces of yourself,
fighting for air.

You are so
enraged,
horrified,
disgusted,
disappointed,
with yourself,
hyperventilating,
tapping,
shaking,
spending
the entire day
swallowing
the unforgiving
shivers
swarming
up your spine.

– *Infested*

The suicidal thoughts
greet you at the bottom
of a pill bottle,

a tiny capsule for
every person's name.

Hold it together. Hold it together. Hold it together.
Hold it together. Hold it together. Hold it together.
Hold it together. Hold it together. Hold it together.
Hold it together. Hold it together. Hold it together.
Hold it together. Hold it together. Hold it together.
Hold it together. Hold it together. Hold it together.
Hold it together. Hold it together. Hold it together.
Hold it together. Hold it together. Hold it together.
Hold it together. Hold it together. Hold it together.
Hold it together. Hold it together. Hold it together.
Hold it together. Hold it together. Hold it together.
Hold it together. Hold it together. Hold it together.
Hold it together. Hold it together. Hold it together.
Hold it together. Hold it together. Hold it together.
Hold it together. Hold it together. Hold it together.
Hold it together. Hold it together. Hold it together.
Hold it together. Hold it together. Hold it together.
Hold it together. Hold it together. Hold it together.
Hold it together. Hold it together. Hold it together.
Hold it together. Hold it together. Hold it together.
Hold it together. Hold it together. Hold it together.
Hold it together. Hold it together. Hold it together.
Hold it together. Hold it together. Hold it together.
Hold it together. Hold it together. Hold it together.
Hold it together. Hold it together. Hold it together.
Hold it together. Hold it together. Hold it together.
Hold it together. Hold it together. Hold it together.

Hold it together. Hold it together. Hold it together.
Hold it together. Hold it together. Hold it together.
Hold it together. Hold it together. Hold it together.
Hold it together. Hold it together. Hold it together.
Hold it together. Hold it together. Hold it together.
Hold it together. Hold it together. Hold it together.
Hold it together. Hold it together. Hold it together.
Hold it together. Hold it together. Hold it together.
Hold it together. Hold it together. Hold it together.
Hold it together. Hold it together. Hold it together.
Hold it together. Hold it together. Hold it together.
Hold it together. Hold it together. Hold it together.
Hold it together. Hold it together. Hold it together.
Hold it together. Hold it together. Hold it together.
Hold it together. Hold it together. Hold it together.
Hold it together. Hold it together. Hold it together.
Hold it together. Hold it together. Hold it together.
Hold it together. Hold it together. Hold it together.
Hold it together. Hold it together. Hold it together.
Hold it together. Hold it together. Hold it together.
Hold it together. Hold it together. Hold it together.
Hold it together. Hold it together. Hold it together.
Hold it together. Hold it together. Hold it together.
Hold it together. Hold it together. Hold it together.
Hold it together. Hold it together. Hold it together.
Hold it together. Hold it together. Hold it together.
Hold it together. Hold it together. Hold it together.

The pills don't make it
down your throat,

instead
they're floating

in the toilet
where they're thrown.

– Flushed Away

Do not hate yourself
for slipping up,

these moments,
whatever they are,
whenever they come,
though they do test you
do not define you.

So please,
do not punish yourself
for slipping up.

You already punish yourself
enough as it is.

Dry your tears,
my love.

You carry a light
so powerful within you
for which no darkness can survive.

– Do Not Give Up

I’m certain my parents didn’t know
what they were doing to me,
their little baby girl,
all smiles, and
warmth, and
joy.

A child deserves
to come into this world loved.

– *We All Do*

I miss,
and love,
and have lost
so many goddamn people,

I don't even know
who I'm writing about anymore.

– *You, and You, and You, and You*

The loneliness within me
feels like the only truth
I have ever known.

That's the paradox of the human spirit,
we were made to be whole
and yet we feel empty.

REGENERATION

I had always wanted to be useful,
and for some time I let other people dictate
whether or not I was
of useful value to them,
but the problem with that was
I was allowing other people
to set the kind of standards
I should have been setting for myself,
and leaving that kind of power
in the wrong hands
will only ever fail you,
and worst of all
leave you feeling more useless
than you ever felt before.

Who were you
before the world broke you
and obscured your sense of compassion?

Perhaps you were a lover
with a heart as bright as gold,
or perhaps you were a fighter
with a spirit fierce and bold,

the thing is
something happened to you,
forcing your truth to fly astray,
and between who you are now
and who you were then

you have somehow
lost your way.

The loneliness
is not your truth,

you have yet
to meet yourself.

The pain has become
parasitic in nature,

it has given nothing,
taken everything,

and you have served
as its host.

You have been holding your heartache hostage,
the most treacherous form
of self-torture.

– The Time Has Come to Let It Go

There are some people in this world
that do not want you to let go of them,
as they benefit from your entrapment,
they do not want you to move on
because their power
rests within your chains.

Release it all,

whatever does not serve
your highest purpose,

whatever does not resonate
with your greatest good,

lure it to the surface,
make your peace,
and release.

You are the only home
that you have,

do not
abandon yourself,

don't you dare
run away.

Forgive yourself,
my dear,

no matter how long it takes,
no matter how hard it seems,
no matter how many times
you have to sit there
with your face in your hands
and tears streaming down
the flushed mounds of your cheeks,

you are going to have to forgive yourself
in order to set your heart free.

And forgive them too,
even if you don't believe
the forgiveness is deserved,
you still deserve to live in peace.

– Practice Mercy

There is no burden
in forgiveness,

the only burden
is in needlessly
holding on to despair.

Letting go of the pain is terrifying
because letting go of the pain
means letting go of everything
you have ever known,

but if you continue to hold on
to what that hurts

there will never be any room
for new adventures,
new people,
or growth.

You cannot un-do what's been done
and although this reality alone
may hurt more than anything
remember that right now
you have the power
not to carry
the weight of the past
forward.

Regret is the act of shaming yourself
in the present

for what has happened
in the past

which ultimately denies you
a future.

– Fight Through It

Anger comes from
taking adversity as a punishment
as opposed to a lesson.

I am too powerful
to let anger speak for me.

You did not
pick all of the wrong people,

your heart simply chose the souls
who've always needed
love the most.

– *The Wounded Healer*

Sometimes it feels as if
people have taken parts of us,

but maybe those parts of us
never really belonged to us
in the first place,

maybe we are all born with parts
solely meant to be given away

– *The Exchange*

Open yourself
to the possibility
that it's okay to let others in,

even if all of your past experiences
have taught you otherwise,

you never know who may change
the entire course of your life.

You cannot hold
the people in your present
accountable for the misguided actions
of the people in your past,

do not confuse
what has happened
for what is currently happening.

– *Things Are Different Now*

Your family didn't know
how to love you,

that doesn't mean
no one ever will.

– *Affirmations to Myself*

Whenever your heart becomes too heavy to bear,
remember the depth of the universe
is not a light load to carry.
Whenever your stomach churns
in the sinking basin of self-doubt,
remember all of the miracles
you have already created,
nothing is impossible.
Whenever you fear you have lost your way,
remember the path toward your destiny
is paved with obstacles built to test you,
but all of the answers you'll ever need
will always be within yourself.
Whenever you feel you are too much,
remind yourself that you are not too much,
you are emotional royalty,
and ethereal wonder,
and you deserve a love
as deep as the endless voids of space itself,
remember the dawn of existence
lives inside your skin,
that you are miraculous
just the way you are,
and you are here because
your life makes this world a better place.

Sensitivity is not for the helpless,
sensitivity is for those brave enough
to feel all of the things
the rest of the world
has shut away.

The trauma
will not be
my identity.

My desire for transformation
far outweighs my desire for ease.

You have to want to fix yourself
before you can actually fix yourself,
any disease or sickness,
if you don't treat it right
it'll kill you,

the first step toward a healthy life
is to want to live,

so figure out the foreign object
that has invaded your being
and tell it that it won't be the end of you.

– *It Can't Be*

The only power
your demons have over you
is the power you continue to afford them.

Only after being broken
do we know what it means to heal.

Destruction is the evolution
of our own creation.

I am taking my life
into my own hands now,

and I will never
hate myself again.

Hatred is the ultimate form
of emptiness.

I needed a way
to fall helplessly
back in love
with myself,
a way to
commit myself
endlessly
to extinguishing
the fire
in my bones.

If they can't love you
in the ways
you need to be loved

then you have to
do it for yourself,

love yourself
in all of the ways
you have never been
loved before.

I gave up
on waiting
for someone
to do it for me,

so I began
writing poems
to myself.

A Poem for All You've Been Through

She was the kind of person
who made you feel important,
like you weren't a mistake
and it didn't matter
how messed up your past was,
who your parents were,
where you've come from
or where you've been.
She was the kind of person to take you by the stars
and remind you that the rest of the world
was not fixated on your pain,
the kind of person who
made you feel perfect for being alive
because you were there with her,
and you were given the opportunity
to help her make herself happy
just as she was given the opportunity
to help you make yourself happy.
She used to say, if you could help make someone happy,
even for just a second,
then you've already done more good
than you could ever possibly know.
And that's exactly why I loved her,
not because she didn't care about my past,
but because she believed in everyone's ability
to change their future.

She is just as powerful
as she is soft,
raw as she is sweet,

there has never been another
heart as loyal as it is
wild and free.

She is not a woman,
she is a miracle.

They could never
beat the love
out of you,

that would be like
trying to beat the light
out of the sun.

– *Impossible*

I am a lover,
I am never going to stop being a lover,
I will do all things in the name of love
and it will be the death of me,

but I will go out fighting
for what I have always believed in,

and this is the only way
I am ever going to live.

Love as hard,
as shamelessly,
and as openly
as possible

without expecting
anyone
or anything
in return.

Unconditional love
doesn't just apply to others,
unconditional love applies to yourself.

Loving yourself
isn't about refusing to change
or failing to remain
critical of who you are,

you should always strive
to be and think better,
to always do your best.

loving yourself
it is about welcoming transformation,

holding yourself accountable
for what needs to be awakened
and what needs to be put to rest.

You do not have to love people less
in order to love yourself more,

do not confuse self-love
with selfishness.

Your self-worth is not embedded
in what they think of you,
who you are is not dictated
by whether or not they like you back,
you were worthy before
they came into your life
and you will still be worthy
if and when they decide to leave,
do not live your days and weeks
based upon who has decided
to give you their attention,
nobody's presence will ever make up
for the absence of your own.

You need you more than anybody.

- *Remember That*

If you feel beautiful enough
in your own skin,

if you feel confident enough
to hold your own head high
despite the world,

that's raw power right there.

– *No One Can Take That from You*

Beauty is
about owning
who you are,
worn skin,
aching bones,
hungry soul,
and all.

I had spent so many years
looking for the answers
in other people,

until I realized
I was the answer,

it was me
who I'd been searching for
all along.

Inner peace comes from
accepting where we are,
understanding that even
our worst circumstances
are purposeful.

Hate cannot harm you
when you are armored with love.

I have laid every seed
of my own misery
before me,

knees bathed
in graveyards of dirt,
heavy with forgiving eyes,

burying it all
deeply into the earth,

with hopes of growing
new life.

Water the garden
of your heart,
fill it with sunlight,
run your fingers
through its vines,
you are eternity in the flesh,
mother nature
in all of her glory.

The root of my home will be deeply adorned
with every flower ever stepped on,
wilted and thrown away,
my windows will be illuminated
with every glimmer of light,
every golden beam
lost to a rainy day,
and my poems will be
grand theatrical stages
for all of the words
we never had the courage to say,
I will bring beauty back from the abyss,
sit in peace with the damaged,
there will never be another darkness,
another wound come to me
left un-kissed.

From this day forward
my life will be
love notes scattered
dancing in the swaying curtains
of all the open windows
I had once nailed shut
in my soul.

– *And I Will Be Free*

Plant flowers
in the empty promises
of the world,

lct forests grow
where they told you
there could be none.

It took me a while
but I belong deeply
to myself now.

In every way
I have broken
I have healed.

TENDERNESS

I had spent so much time healing myself,
so much practice giving to myself,
the day had finally come
for me to bring intimacy to those around me,
to learn how to love other people
in all of the ways I had finally learned
how to love myself.

– *New Pathways*

A ship is built for the roaring sea
not the serenity of the harbor,

understand that you will get lost
and night will fall,

but you will always
have the stars.

You do not have to be fearless,
but you can learn to fear less.

One day you are going to meet somebody
who will take the taste of blood
right out of your mouth,
buff away those sleepy purple bruises
of broken violets beneath your eyes,
mend all of those nasty scrapes
inside your head,
they are going to make you feel
like somebody in this world
actually gives a damn about you.
They are going to pick you up
and never put you back down.
That's right,
you are going to meet somebody
who will never drop you
just to watch you break.
They are going to be every impossible thing
you never thought existed for you,
all of the happy endings you never had,
they are going to accept your flaws
and deserve you
just as much as you deserve them,
and they will love you,
all of you.

– *Always*

Love is not impossible.

– Even for You

The first time
he touches you
leaves blossom
at your sides,

ripening you
like sweet cherries,
honeysuckle
and wine,

dripping sugar
like warm tongues
melting your insides.

Making love to you
is meeting God
within myself.

– Healing

I collapsed into you
the same way the universe collapsed into itself,
we went from nothingness to somethingness
in a matter of moments,
broken down into milliseconds,
spread out over the course of eternity
in ways we couldn't even touch if we tried,
that's what falling in love with you was like,
it was every subatomic particle within me
being blasted forward into re-existence,
expanding outwardly and infinitely
all at once,
in each direction,
forever.
Falling in love with you
was just like that,
like being resurrected from the dark,
born again from the night
to a sky full of stars.

"You are not from this world,"
he says.

"You are right," I say.
"I am from a world of my own."

– *Ethereal*

He is an artist
at making love,

the way he breathes
life back into you,

worshiping you,

making it deeply so
the only word you remember
is his name.

My body has always felt
like the same horrid mess,
the same empty canvas of bitterness
I have grown to know so well,
but with your body
painted next to mine
I have come to feel
like a masterpiece.

– *Naked*

I was terrified
that loving someone
would un-do all of the hard work
I had already put into myself,

years' worth of practice,
patience and discipline
all annihilated in an instant,

I wasn't sure if I was ready
to accept the possible repercussions
of another broken heart,

I had hardly survived
my last.

– *The Nature of Chernobyl*

I was always taught
love is pain,

but love is not pain,
pain is pain,

love is
the liberation.

Somehow
the whole world
makes sense
when we're together.

– *When It's Only Me and You*

You are the light,
everything else is the tunnel.

You taught me tenderness
is asking the right questions,
reading in between my mind
and the lines of my palms,

you asked about my mother,
and I told you
I had always been on my own,

so you asked
about my future.

– *Where Was I Going to Go?*

"When did you realize
you wanted to be with me?"
he asked.

"That night on the beach
I saw you walking all alone,"
I said.
"And you?"

"Before I met you," he said.
"I have always wanted to know
someone like you."

You are all
of the possibilities
I never thought
existed for me,

every good thing
about this world,

even on the days
you feel you are not.

I will always want
your heart to feel safe with me.

I would endure
my whole life over again,

relive every horrific agony,
every snarling detail

if it meant one day
it would bring me to you.

You are my happy place.

I have never known
  another love like yours.

– And I Don't Care To

You make me feel
the unthinkable.

You will always
be enough for me.

I needed someone
to meet me as deeply
as I had met myself,

someone who only visited
the surface

but lived and flourished
in the depths.

"I love you," I say.
"I will reassure you of this
as many times as you need."

"And what if you grow tired?"
He asks.

"Then I will grab us both a pillow,"
I say.

"And what if I hurt you?"
He fears.

"We are going to hurt each other,"
I confess.
"Most times we won't mean to."

"And what if you leave?"
He worries.

"Then I hope
you will come with me."

People want to feel free
to be themselves,
liberty is the foundation
of happiness and love,
if you love somebody
and want them to be happy
release the idea of ownership,
do not cage anyone in
but encourage them to fly,
because if someone really does love you
then nothing in this world
is ever going to make them leave,
not all the freedom imaginable,
not even a pair of wings.

Create a love that transcends
and carries you beyond the periphery.

– *Metaphysical*

Love is not about being invincible,
love is about vulnerability.

Be with someone
who understands you
on the days you do not
understand yourself,

someone who reassures you
that you are not a catastrophe,

even when you feel
like a storm.

Your heart
is a divine force
of nature.

– *Do Not Underestimate Its Magnitude*

You are not *too much*,
the earth doesn't complain
about the weight of thc ocean,
the sun doesn't contain
the intensity of its heat,
the ocean doesn't cower
beneath the might of a full moon,
you are not *too much*,
you just haven't found the right arms
strong enough to hold you.

You do not need to be
in the most perfect place of your life
or the best version of yourself possible
in order for somebody to love you,

you can be loved right now,
completely.

– Just as You Are

Time means nothing
to our hearts,

I have gone nowhere
with people I've known for years,

and have traveled through millennia
with people I've only known for a night.

Every relationship you have
will be different.

– *Love is Shapeless*

Bring intimacy
into your friendships,
your friends need you too,

they require just as much attention,
support, and consideration,
as your romantic partners do.

Your friends
are also your soulmates.

– Love and Take Care of Them Too

My best friend isn't like a flower,
flowers grow peacefully,
my best friend is more like a mountain,
she has gained her magnificence
through earthly instability,
through the shifting tectonic plates
in her soul.
Don't get me wrong,
flowers are beautiful,
but not a single daffodil,
lilac,
carnation,
or dahlia
will ever compare
to the sky conquering altitude
of her imperfect ridges.

– *S.M.*

Treasure the people who inspire you,
the one's who remind you
why it is you held on
for so long.

Love will always
find its way back to us,

it is the inescapable
law of our universe.

You helped
revive my faith
in love,

showed me
even the most solemn hearts
can still move on.

My love for you
was not a result of your perfection,
my love for you was simply
a reflection of everything
that shines, darkens, hardens,
and is born again within you,
the perfectly imperfect
person that is you.
I am simply thankful for the way
our paths brushed shoulders,
and despite whether or not
we continue to be a part of
each other's lives
I will always remember you
and hold you close to my heart
for helping me
more than you will ever know.

– *Que Sera Sera*

You never really know
just how much
you mean to someone

and you never really know
just how much
your presence has
impacted a person's life.

Being with you was
the softest,
most peaceful thing
that has ever
happened
to me.

All stories
come to an end,

but the lessons,
magic, and wonder
they've taught

live on within us
forever.

You came gentle
in the night,
soft with open palms,
like catching fireflies
in the rocky canyons
of my heart,
showing me my light
would always illuminate
the dark,
and just like the fireflies
and the stars,
you were gone peacefully
with the moon,

magically
at dawn.

I owe my life to all of the people
who have loved me back to myself.

– Thank You

SALVATION

I am the personification
of my entire life's experiences,

I am not my body
I am my story.

My journey has not only lead me
outward through the world
but inward through myself,

for every mountain climbed
there has been another
emotional height conquered,

for every ocean touched
there has been another
aching wound healed,

I want to continue
to be moved so deeply
by the sights of this world

that I myself forever dream
in the kind of colors
that can only be earned.

The abyss gave me
an understanding of the light
no other force of nature could supply.

– *Awakening*

My awakening was not gentle,
winter did not gradually fade
into the warmth of spring,

my awakening was brutally
staring into the abyss,

as the abyss brutally
stared back into me.

In all of the places
you have felt eternal night
the sun shall rise again.

Life has a way of sensing strength,
the way it pushes us toward the fiery pits
of our own innermost fears,

bringing us face first
against the horrors
of our own burning flames,

just to see who will and will not
make it through alive.

– *The Evolution of Our Consciousness*

I cannot promise
the healing will be pretty,
that the healing will always feel
right, worthwhile, or good,

but the healing will be healing,
and you will rise again
despite the world.

– *Ashes and Scars*

Overcoming the pain
will not be done in one day,

it takes time to harness the power
needed to break the pain.

– *Gentle Strides*

Becoming is a day-by-day process,
do not intimidate yourself
with ideas of tomorrow,
for it has not yet arrived,

and do not depress yourself
with memories of the past,
for it too has already made its way,

pause, and bring your awareness
to the very moment at hand,

feel yourself here,

reading
each
and every
word

written for you
on this page.

– *Presence*

I am always learning,
continually expanding,
forever changing,
I am never obligated
to be the same person
I was all of those years ago
and I am never obligated
to be the same person
I was last night
before I went to sleep,

I will never be complete,
there is no final phase for me,
no permanent state
of being.

It is right what they say,
that you must learn
how to stay true
to yourself,

but first
you must learn
what your truth is.

My truth is to contribute
as little suffering as is possible
to the entirety of this world,

to fill myself
and everything I touch
with compassion and love.

– *Abundance*

Negative self-fulfilling prophecies are dangerous,
when we convince ourselves we are unlovable,
too complicated, beyond being understood,
that our lives have and always will be
too messed up to move on from,
that's when we actually need
to comfort and reassure ourselves the most,
when our realities become twisted
by poisonous environments,
toxic relationships,
or bad habits and choices,
it's hard to see the repetitive patterns
for what they are,
but your entire life belongs to you,
treat yourself the way
you treat the people you love,
do that for yourself,
allow yourself to feel something good,
it's okay to prove yourself wrong,
to show yourself maybe things can get better,

you are not just chaos,
I promise.

You are beautiful,
you do not need any further proof
than the practiced understanding
that you are simply alive,
breathing and being,
a cosmic wonder of miracles
etched into your skin,
billions of years beating
to the rhythm of your heart,
your eyes the raging mirrors
of every intergalactic river,

the royal kingdom is you,
you are the flesh and blood
of the universe's fortune.

Your life didn't begin
at conception,
your life began
thirteen billion years ago
with the rest of everything else
in this universe,
you are just as old
as everything you ever came from.

It is your nature
to transform.

Each of us has
a history to tell,
a lesson to teach,
a secret to exchange,
a journey that has
transformed our souls
into the everchanging forces
they are today.

Everyone's story is unique
and everyone's story deserves to be heard.

– *To Grow and Learn With One Another*

We live in a world that has conditioned us
to feel shameful about our pain,
to smile through the horrors,
to keep our festering wounds locked away,
as if confronting adversity
somehow makes us irritating,
burdensome and less worthy as people,
but that simply couldn't be
further from the truth,

being open about our heartache
is one of the bravest,
most life-saving things
we can help each other do.

– Hand in Hand

To break
is to be human.

The biggest mistake
we can make in this world
is convincing ourselves
we do not need each other.

We're here to love
and help one another,

that's it,
that's the secret,

the grand mystery
behind it all.

No one should be
forced to keep
the reality of their pain
hidden behind closed doors,
doors keep people out,
and what we need to start doing
is letting each other in.

Tune into the rhythm
of those around you,

hold space for them,
ask them about their day,

you never know
who may be pretending
everything is okay.

We empower people
by listening.

Receiving help does not
invalidate your independence,
even the stars need the night to shine.

Part of growing up is learning
how to be honest about who you are,
it's about developing enough confidence
to tell yourself what you really want,
how you really feel,
where you really want to go,

it's about who you strive to be
and it's about sharing this gift
of self-discovery with others,

about helping the people around you
learn how to be honest with themselves, too.

Growing up means growing out
of all of the old stuff
that doesn't fit you anymore,

dispose of those
hand-me-down thoughts,

clothe your mind
with ideas that fit.

It’s not about
what I believe in,

it’s about
all of the things

I don’t believe in
anymore.

The right relationships will help you
set the standard
for your own self-worth,
and once you have experienced
this kind of raw honesty,
respect, and appreciation
you will never settle
for anything less.

– *Building Each Other Up*

We spend so much time looking for a key
to unlock the door to happiness,
but the door to happiness
has never been locked,
the door to happiness
has always been open
and it will always stay open
for anyone willing enough
to seek prosperity
within and without themselves,

there is no special key,
no impenetrable lock,

happiness simply begins
with allowing yourself
to step through the light
of an already open door.

You are always
right where you need to be,

if you were meant to be
anywhere else

then you would be
anywhere else,

but you are not anywhere else,
you are here.

Happiness is here
and now.

Coming into yourself
is the unlearning
of every deception
keeping you
from remembering
all of which lies within.

I pried myself open to the possibilities
in the name of becoming
something more.

Jumped whenever
I felt like holding myself back,
took the risk whenever
I felt like playing it safe,
spoke my heart whenever
I felt like swallowing my truth,
rose to my feet whenever
I felt chained to the floor.

I challenged myself repeatedly
to do the things
I was taught never to do
because I refused to live a life
suffering in the never-changing
safety of my comfort zone.

By embracing the inevitable
we embrace change,
to embrace change
is to dismantle fear of the future,
to dismantle fear of the future
is to bring power into the now,
to bring power into the now
is to liberate your soul from excess,
to liberate your soul from excess
is to set yourself free.

Watch the doors
open themselves to you

as you choose in favor of
what calls to your soul.

Taking your life
into your own hands
is a scary thought,
to liberate your mind
and become truly
responsible for yourself,
but the beauty in that is
once you become
responsible for yourself
you are in control
of how you consciously think,
where you consciously go,
and you get to decide
what is and isn't worth
suffering for.

You are the universe
taking its destiny
into its own hands.

Look closely at the pain patterns in your life:

Where does sorrow manifest in your body?
Is it your back, your throat, your chest?
Which thoughts hurt you most?
Are you allowing your mind to rest?
Where is your suffering rooted?
Is it in family, relationships, or friends?
Perhaps it is in yourself,
you're feeling lonely, anxious, or depressed.
What are these cycles
constantly moving through you?
What are these patterns trying to teach?
Bring awareness to what hurts you,
then forgive, let go, and make your peace.

Listen to your body,
for it speaks an ancient language.

You have the power to improve your life
with the practice of gratitude,
by reminding yourself to be thankful,
to appreciate your surroundings,
to love the people who love you
and to continue to love the ones who don’t,
love everybody actually,
let your presence on this planet
be a revolution in and of itself,
a rebellion against all odds,
a movement against hate,
apathy and negativity,
listen to yourself,
become your own guide,
but don’t forget about the others,
there are still plenty of people out there
who are still in the same position
you once were,
and if you truly want
to make a difference on this earth
then you will continue to help those people
whenever you can, too.

Be the light
the world says
no longer exists.

Own your kindness,
empathy is not a downfall.

Either you're going to take charge
and change your life as you please

or life is going to take charge
and change you as it pleases.

– For Better, For Worse

You are only as capable,

only as jaded,
only as brave,
only as broken,
only as loving

as you believe yourself to be.

– *Choose Wisely*

Your life happened
the way it's happened
for a reason

and the reason is yours
to decide.

I have come
such a long way
with myself,

yet I am
more me

than I could have
ever imagined.

Meet yourself far,
at the ends of your own world.

We all have what it takes
to change the narrative of our lives.

It's the art of re-creating yourself,
reclaiming your future
in the name of not being boring,
in the name of doing something
catastrophically worthwhile,

I don't want what anyone else has,
what I want is a story to tell,
where I'm going is anywhere,
who I need is me.

It is never too late
to meet yourself.

Your soul is looking for you.

I am so grateful to have met you here,
through these words,
on this page.
I want to thank you
for listening to a story
I never thought I'd have the courage to tell,
for holding me with love,
for picking this book.
You have some of my most treasured secrets with you now,
I have enchanted them to keep you safe.
There are so many more important smiles to be had,
so many more life changing adventures that await.
I am blessing you with the warmth of a thousand suns,
filling you with the light of a trillion stars,
so that you may always find your way home,
so that you may always illuminate the dark.

– From This Day Forward
Anna

33975947R00179

Made in the USA
Lexington, KY
16 March 2019